MasterChef
Quick
Wins

Contents

45 Minutes and Under

15 Minutes and Under

Roast figs with Gorgonzola and honey vinegar sauce

Alison Reynolds @ quarter-finalist

Preparation time 5 minutes   **Cooking time** 5 minutes   **Serves 4**

Ingredients

8 ripe figs

salt and freshly ground black pepper

100g (3½oz) Gorgonzola cheese, cut into equal-sized cubes

4 tsp red wine vinegar

2 tbsp clear honey

85g (3oz) rocket, to garnish

Method

1 Preheat the grill to hot and grease a baking tray. Place the figs in the baking tray, cut a cross in the top of each, season with salt and pepper, and grill for 2 minutes or until warmed through.

2 Place a cube of cheese on the top of each fig and grill for a further 2–3 minutes, or until the cheese starts to melt and colour.

3 Meanwhile, make the honey sauce by whisking together the vinegar and honey in a bowl.

4 To serve, place 2 figs on each plate, drizzle over the sauce, and garnish with the rocket.

Warm Mediterranean salad with braised fennel and pancetta croutons

Matt James @ Celebrity quarter-finalist

Preparation time 15 minutes   **Cooking time** 15 minutes   **Serves 4**

Ingredients

1 radicchio

100g (3½oz) watercress

16 cherry tomatoes, halved

12 black olives, pitted and halved

4 tbsp olive oil

sea salt and freshly ground black pepper

2 fennel bulbs, finely sliced

12 juniper berries, crushed

125g (4½oz) pancetta, cubed

1 tbsp fennel seeds, toasted and crushed

Method →

Method

1 Tear the radicchio and watercress leaves into a large salad bowl. Add the cherry tomatoes and olives and then mix the whole lot together with 2 tbsp olive oil and a pinch of salt and pepper.

2 Brush or drizzle the remaining olive oil over the fennel slices. Put a non-stick frying pan and a griddle pan on high heat.

3 When the frying pan is hot, add the juniper berries and, a minute or so later, throw in the pancetta cubes and toss them around until golden. There is no need to add any extra oil; the fat from the pork is more than enough. Transfer to kitchen paper to absorb the excess fat. Discard the juniper berries and leave the pancetta croutons to rest.

4 When the griddle is very hot, add the fennel slices. For a warm but crunchy bite, cook each side for about 3 minutes.

5 To serve, make a bed of salad on each plate, then lay the fennel on top and sprinkle over the pancetta croutons and the fennel seeds.

Smoked trout with celeriac and apple remoulade and mustard dressing

inspired by **Jamie Barnett** ℗ **Professionals quarter-finalist**

Preparation time 10 minutes   **Serves 4**

Ingredients

½ celeriac, about 250g (9oz)

2 Cox's apples

1 tbsp grain mustard

6 tbsp olive oil

1 tbsp white wine vinegar

sea salt and freshly ground black pepper

4 fillets hot-smoked Wiltshire trout

Method

1 Peel and coarsely grate the celeriac. Then peel and grate the apple and combine with the celeriac in a serving bowl.

2 Whisk together the mustard, oil, and vinegar and season well, then use to dress the celeriac and apple.

3 Divide the dressed salad between 4 plates and top with the smoked trout fillets.

Thai prawn soup with lemongrass

Iwan Thomas @ Celebrity finalist

Preparation time 10 minutes   **Cooking time** 15 minutes   **Serves 4**

Ingredients

16 large raw tiger prawns, shells on

1 litre (1¾ pints) chicken stock

2 stalks fresh lemongrass, lightly pounded, cut into 2.5cm (1in) lengths

50g (1¾oz) sliced fresh galangal

10 kaffir lime leaves, shredded

500g (1lb 2oz) straw mushrooms, halved or whole

4 tbsp nam pla (Thai fish sauce)

3 tbsp nam prik pao (chilli paste in oil)

4 tbsp lime juice

5 crushed fresh Thai (bird's eye) chillies

To garnish

10g (¼oz) coriander, torn

1 small red pepper, deseeded and cut into fine ribbons

Method

1 Wash the prawns and shell them without removing the tails. Devein them if necessary.

2 Bring the chicken stock to the boil in a large saucepan. Add the lemongrass, galangal, and lime leaves.

3 Bring back to the boil, then add the straw mushrooms, nam pla, nam prik pao, and lime juice. Add the prawns and fresh chillies.

4 As soon as the prawns turn pink (about 2 minutes), serve the soup, garnished with the coriander and strips of red pepper.

TECHNIQUE

How to devein and butterfly prawns

1 If the intestinal vein running down the back of a prawn is black, cut lightly along it with a paring knife. Remove the vein with the knife tip, and rinse the prawn under cold running water.

2 To butterfly a prawn, cut along the deveined back and splay it open, but take care not to cut all the way through. Rinse under cold running water and pat dry with kitchen paper.

Seared beef with cucumber and poppy seed salad

Cassandra Williams @ quarter-finalist

Preparation time 15 minutes   **Cooking time** 2 minutes   **Serves 4**

Ingredients

1 cucumber

1 tbsp rice vinegar

2 tbsp sunflower oil

1 tbsp poppy seeds

1 tbsp caster sugar

1 mild red chilli, deseeded and finely sliced

bunch of coriander, chopped

1 tsp coriander seeds

1 tsp cumin seeds

freshly ground black pepper

1 tsp sea salt

150g (5½oz) fillet of beef

2 tsp sesame seeds

1 tbsp olive oil

handful of purple basil and radish sprouts, to serve

For the dressing

2 tsp olive oil

1 tsp sesame oil

1 tbsp rice vinegar

1 tbsp light soy sauce

Method

1 Halve cucumber lengthways and remove the seeds. Finely slice and put in a bowl with the rice vinegar, 1 tbsp sunflower oil and the poppy seeds, sugar, chilli, and coriander. Mix well and place in the fridge.

2 Crush coriander and cumin seeds with black pepper and sea salt in a pestle and mortar. Trim excess fat or sinew off the fillet, then roll in the crushed spices until coated. Put the sesame seeds on a plate.

3 Heat the olive oil in a frying pan until hot. Add the fillet and sear on each side for about 1 minute. Remove from the pan. Roll in the sesame seeds, then leave to rest for 10 minutes.

4 For the dressing, whisk the oils with the rice vinegar and the soy sauce, then season. Just before serving, toss the basil and radish sprouts into the dressing until they are lightly and evenly coated, then remove.

5 To serve, finely slice the beef and arrange on a plate, positioning slightly to one side. Put a mound of the cucumber salad on the other side and then lightly place the basil and sprouts around the plate.

Mackerel tartare and smoked mackerel pâté with cucumber papardelle

David Coulson @ Professionals finalist

Preparation time 15 minutes   **Serves 4**

Ingredients

100g (3½oz) fresh mackerel, filleted, all bones removed

30g (1oz) creamed horseradish sauce

200g (7oz) crème fraîche

2 tbsp fresh dill, finely chopped

1 tsp lemon thyme leaves

juice of 2 lemons

100g (3½oz) smoked mackerel

3 tbsp double cream

1 egg yolk

1 medium cucumber

1 tsp apple vinegar

sprigs of thyme and dill, to garnish

Method →

Method

1 For the mackerel tartare, flake the mackerel and mix with the horseradish sauce, 150g (5½oz) of the crème fraîche, 1 tbsp of the dill, the lemon thyme, and half the lemon juice. Season and chill.

2 To make the pâté, blend the smoked mackerel, double cream, egg yolk, and remaining crème fraîche until smooth, using a hand blender or food processor.

3 Using a vegetable peeler, remove the skin from the cucumber and then cut long, thin strips of flesh using the same peeler. Mix in a bowl with the apple vinegar and the remaining lemon juice and dill.

4 To serve, divide the mackerel tartare between 4 plates, spooning it down the length of the plate. At one end top with a spoon of smoked mackerel pâté, then garnish with cucumber papardelle and sprigs of dill and thyme.

St Emilion au chocolat

William Leigh semi-finalist

Preparation time 10 minutes **Serves 4**

Ingredients

100g (3½oz) dark chocolate (70% cocoa), plus extra for decoration

100ml (3½fl oz) whole milk

50g (1¾oz) unsalted butter

50g (1¾oz) caster sugar

1 egg yolk

125g (4½oz) ratafia or amaretti biscuits, crushed

4 tsp brandy

double cream, to serve

Method

1 Put the chocolate and milk in a saucepan and gently heat until the chocolate has melted.

2 Put the butter, sugar, and egg yolk in a food processor and blend, and then pour into the chocolate mixture, continuously stirring.

3 With a piece of kitchen paper, wipe around four 7cm (2¾in) ring moulds with some softened butter, and place onto serving plates. Divide the crushed biscuits into the base of each of the rings. Sprinkle 1 tsp of the brandy over each of the bases and then carefully pour in the chocolate, dividing evenly between the 4 rings. Leave to chill in the fridge for 1 hour.

4 Remove the puddings from the rings and serve with double cream.

Pan-fried baby squid with sun-blushed tomato and rocket

Sharon Maughan Celebrity semi-finalist

Preparation time 10 minutes   **Cooking time** 5 minutes   **Serves 4**

Ingredients

450g (1lb) baby squid, cleaned and tentacles discarded

salt

2 tsp piment d'Espelette powder (or 1 tsp each of hot and sweet smoked paprika)

3 tbsp olive oil

18 sunblush tomatoes

3 garlic cloves, finely chopped

1 tbsp chopped flat-leaf parsley

50g (1¾oz) rocket leaves

1 red chilli, deseeded and finely chopped (optional)

Method

1 Slice the squid into 5mm (¼in) thick rings and pat dry on kitchen paper. Season the squid with salt to taste, and add the piment d'Espelette.

2 Heat a frying pan until very hot. Add the olive oil and then the squid. Cook for no more than 1 minute, until the squid is golden in colour. Turn over and add the tomatoes, garlic, and parsley.

3 Cook for a further minute, then remove from the heat and serve immediately, garnished with rocket leaves.

4 For some extra heat, add some finely chopped red chilli just before serving.

Savoury toasts

Ruth Goodman @ Celebrity contestant

Preparation time 10minutes   **Cooking time** 10–15 minutes   **Serves 4**

Ingredients

4 slices of sourdough bread for toast

½ tbsp olive oil

1 whole lamb's liver, deveined and cut into small cubes

1 tsp fennel seeds

salt and freshly ground black pepper

50g (1¾oz) butter

3 tbsp double cream

tiny sprigs of thyme leaves, to garnish

Method

1 Preheat the oven to 190°C (375°F/Gas 5). Drizzle the sliced bread with the olive oil and lay out on a baking tray. Place in the oven and bake for 5–8 minutes, checking regularly until the slices have turned golden brown. Remove from the oven and place on the serving plates.

2 Meanwhile, place the pieces of liver in a bowl. Add the fennel seeds and a generous grinding of black pepper. Mix together.

3 Melt the butter in a frying pan over medium to high heat. When the butter begins to foam, add the liver and spice mix. Fry for 2–3 minutes, turning so that all sides are browned evenly. (If you do not have a large frying pan, this may need to be done in batches.)

4 Once the liver is browned, add the cream to the pan, bring to the boil, and simmer for 2–3 minutes. Taste and season if necessary.

5 Serve the liver on the toast, and garnish with fresh sprigs of thyme.

30 Minutes and Under

Wild mushroom bruschetta

Helen Cristofoli @ quarter-finalist

Preparation time 10minutes   **Cooking time** 20 minutes   **Serves 4**

Ingredients

8 x 5cm (2in) thick slices from a baguette, cut on the diagonal

3 tbsp olive oil

sea salt and freshly ground black pepper

1 shallot, thinly sliced

1 garlic clove, crushed

200g (7oz) mixed wild and chestnut mushrooms, sliced

100ml (3½fl oz) white wine

2 tbsp chopped parsley, to garnish

Method

1 Preheat the oven to 200°C (400°F/Gas 6). Lightly brush both sides of the baguette slices with some of the olive oil, sprinkle very lightly with salt, place on a baking sheet, and bake for 8–10 minutes or until crisp and lightly browned at the edges.

2 Heat the remaining olive oil in a frying pan and sauté the shallot for 2–3 minutes or until beginning to soften. Add the garlic and mushrooms, a generous pinch of salt, and a good grind of pepper and,

keeping the pan over high heat, sauté for about 10 minutes until the mushrooms release their juices and begin to reabsorb them. Continue to sauté until the mushrooms are golden brown.

3 Add the wine and boil for about 1 minute until the wine is absorbed into the mushrooms. Check the seasoning.

4 To serve, place 2 bruschetta on each serving plate and top each with the mushroom mixture. Garnish with the parsley.

Warmed goat's cheese salad with walnuts

Louise Colley @ quarter-finalist

Preparation time 5 minutes   **Cooking time** 15 minutes   **Serves 4**

Ingredients

300g (10oz) round goat's cheeses

85g (3oz) walnut pieces, toasted and slightly crushed

150g (5½oz) rocket leaves

½ tsp salt

1 tsp walnut or olive oil

For the dressing

2 tbsp pomegranate molasses

2 tbsp lemon juice

6 tbsp olive oil

1 pomegranate

Method

1 To make the dressing, whisk together the molasses, lemon juice, and oil. Slice the pomegranate in half and, with a wooden spoon, hit the side of the pomegranate halves to release the seeds from the shell more easily. Add the seeds to the dressing, then set to one side until ready to serve. (Pomegranate molasses can be difficult to get hold of, so to make your own, mix together 3 tbsp caster sugar with 250ml (8fl oz) pomegranate juice and the juice of 1 lemon.)

2 Preheat the grill to low. Cut the goat's cheese rounds into slices, about 2cm (¾in) thick, and transfer to a baking sheet. Top with the toasted walnuts and place under the grill for about 1 minute to warm through, until the cheese starts to soften but still holds its shape.

3 Put the rocket into a large bowl, season with the salt, and add the walnut or olive oil to coat the leaves.

4 To assemble, place a handful of rocket in the centre of each plate and place 2 to 3 slices of the goat's cheese on top. Finally, drizzle the pomegranate dressing around the plate.

Fresh pea soup with white truffle oil and Parmesan crisps

Jonny Stevenson @ finalist

Preparation time 15 minutes   **Cooking time** 20 minutes   **Serves 4**

Ingredients

2 tbsp sea salt

2 tbsp sugar

1.8kg (4lb) freshly shelled garden peas, kept chilled

salt and white pepper

8 rounded tsp freshly grated Parmesan cheese

4 tsp white truffle oil

Method →

Method

1 Bring 1 litre (1¾ pints) water to the boil in a large saucepan and add the salt and sugar. When the water is at a rapid boil, add the chilled peas. Cover immediately – it is important that you raise the water temperature as quickly as possible. Cook the peas until tender, about 6–9 minutes.

2 Drain the peas, reserving the cooking water. Place the cooked peas in a blender or food processor and pulse for 1–2 minutes, adding a little of the cooking water.

3 Pass the pea purée through a sieve, discarding the solids and remembering to scrape the bottom of the sieve. Adjust the consistency by adding enough cooking water to the sieved pea purée to give a smooth, silky soup. Season with salt and pepper.

4 Preheat the oven to 180°C (350°F/Gas 4). To make the crisps, put the 8 rounded tsp of grated Parmesan cheese onto a baking sheet lined with baking parchment. Flatten them out into rounds and bake for about 5–10 minutes. Remove them from the oven, then, while they are still warm, lift them with a palette knife and drape them over a rolling pin so that they set in a rounded shape.

5 If necessary, reheat the soup in a pan. Add the truffle oil. Ladle the soup into 4 white cups or bowls and gently place the Parmesan crisps alongside.

Mussels à la provençale

inspired by **Luciana Byrne**  quarter-finalist

Preparation time 10 minutes **Cooking time** 15 minutes **Serves 4**

Ingredients

3 tbsp olive oil

1 onion, finely chopped

2 garlic cloves, finely chopped

1 celery stick, finely chopped

4 vine-ripened tomatoes, skinned, deseeded, and chopped

1 bay leaf

1 tsp thyme leaves

200ml (7fl oz) dry white wine

2kg (4½lb) live mussels, cleaned

2 tbsp chopped flat-leaf parsley

2 tbsp chopped basil

Method

1 Heat the oil in a large saucepan, big enough to take all the mussels, and soften the onion, garlic, and celery.

2 Add the chopped tomatoes, bay leaf, and thyme, then pour in the wine and bring to the boil. Tip in the mussels, place the lid on the pan, and turn up the heat, shaking every now and then.

3 Steam the mussels for 4–6 minutes or until most of them are open; discard those that aren't.

4 Stir through the parsley and basil before serving in warmed bowls.

Seasonal salad of broad beans, courgettes, feta, and mint

Helen Gilmour @ quarter-finalist

Preparation time 30 minutes   **Cooking time** 5 minutes   **Serves 4**

Ingredients

20g (¾oz) mint leaves

150ml (5fl oz) olive oil

pinch of caster sugar

3 courgettes

sea salt and freshly ground black pepper

250g (9oz) shelled broad beans

juice of 1 lemon

100g (3½oz) rocket leaves

100g (3½oz) barrel-aged feta cheese

Method →

Method

1 Put half of the mint leaves, 100ml (3½fl oz) of the olive oil, and the sugar in a blender and whizz to mix together. Transfer to a bowl, refrigerate, and leave to infuse.

2 With a wide vegetable peeler, shave the courgettes into strips. Place in a colander, sprinkle with sea salt, and leave to drain.

3 Cook the broad beans in boiling water for 5 minutes until tender, drain, and refresh in iced water.

4 Meanwhile, in a small bowl, mix together the lemon juice and remaining olive oil to make a dressing. Season with salt and pepper.

5 Strain the mint-oil dressing through a fine sieve, if you wish.

6 To assemble the salad, drain the broad beans and transfer to a salad bowl. Rinse the courgettes, drain them on kitchen paper, and add to the broad beans. Then add the rocket leaves and crumble in the feta. Finely slice the remaining mint leaves and stir through the salad and dress with the lemon-oil dressing, adding seasoning.

7 Serve drizzled with the mint-oil dressing.

How to finely slice herbs

To chop the leaves of herbs with tender stalks like basil, and avoid bruising them, roll the leaves together into a tight bunch. Holding the bunch of leaves steady with one hand, slice across them with a sharp chef's knife to create fine shreds. Using the knife in a rocking motion, chop the leaves finely, turning them by 90 degrees halfway through.

Mussels with chipotles and coriander

inspired by **Thomasina Miers** @ champion

Preparation time 15 minutes   **Cooking time** 15 minutes   **Serves 4**

Ingredients

25g (scant 1oz) butter

2 shallots, finely chopped

2 garlic cloves, finely chopped

1 tbsp chipotle chillies in oil

200ml (7fl oz) dry white wine

2kg (4½lb) live mussels, cleaned

handful of coriander leaves, roughly chopped

75ml (2½fl oz) double cream

Method

1 Melt the butter in a large saucepan, big enough to take all the mussels, and sweat the shallots and garlic over low heat to soften but not colour.

2 Stir in the chipotle chillies, then pour in the wine and bring to the boil. Tip in the mussels, place the lid on the pan, and turn up the heat, shaking every now and then. Steam the mussels for 4–6 minutes until most of them are open; discard those that aren't.

3 Finally, stir through the coriander and cream before serving in warmed bowls.

Sesame-crusted tuna with horseradish mousse

Christopher Souto @ semi-finalist

Preparation time 20 minutes   **Cooking time** 4–5 minutes   **Serves 4**

Ingredients

700g (1½lb) yellow fin tuna

3 tbsp light soy sauce

2 tsp sesame oil

3 tbsp vegetable oil

2 tsp Dijon mustard

3 tbsp olive oil, plus extra for cooking

1 tbsp white wine vinegar

salt and freshly ground black pepper

100ml (3½fl oz) double cream

3 tsp creamed horseradish

2 tbsp black sesame seeds

2 tbsp white sesame seeds

50g (1¾oz) rocket

50g (1¾oz) watercress

Method

1 Cut the tuna into 4 square steaks and put in a single layer in a dish. Mix together the soy sauce, sesame oil, vegetable oil, and 1 tsp of the mustard. Pour over the tuna and leave for 2 hours, or overnight, in the fridge.

2 In a bowl, combine the remaining mustard with the olive oil and the vinegar and blend to make a vinaigrette. Season with salt and pepper to taste.

3 To make the horseradish mousse, combine the cream with the creamed horseradish and then whip using an electric hand whisk until light and fluffy. Season with salt and pepper to taste.

4 Mix together the black and white sesame seeds on a plate. Drain the marinade from the tuna steaks and roll them in the seeds. Add a dash of olive oil to a frying pan and, over high heat, cook the steaks for 2 minutes on each side.

5 Serve each of the tuna steaks with a quenelle of mousse and the rocket and watercress salad lightly tossed in the vinaigrette.

Pan-fried sea bream with roasted tomatoes and a fennel salad

Andy Oliver @ finalist

Preparation time 15 minutes   **Cooking time** 20 minutes   **Serves 4**

Ingredients

20 vine-ripened cherry tomatoes

salt and freshly ground black pepper

4 garlic cloves, unpeeled, lightly crushed

2 sprigs of rosemary

150ml (5fl oz) olive oil

pinch of dried chilli flakes

2 small bulbs fennel, with fronds if possible

squeeze of lemon juice

a few fresh basil leaves, finely shredded

4 sea bream fillets

Method

1 Preheat the oven to 180°C (350°F/Gas 4).

2 Season the tomatoes with salt and pepper and place in a roasting tin with the garlic, rosemary, 120ml (4fl oz) olive oil, and a sprinkling of chilli flakes. Put in the oven and roast for 15–20 minutes.

3 Meanwhile, shave the fennel finely on a mandolin and mix with a pinch of salt, 1 tbsp oil, and a squeeze of lemon juice. Keep fronds aside for garnish.

4 For the dressing, take some oil from tomato roasting tin and allow to cool. Add a squeeze of lemon juice and adjust the seasoning. Add the basil.

5 Trim the bream fillets and score the skin finely. Heat a frying pan until hot and add the remaining olive oil. Season the fish and pan-fry it skin-side down until the skin is crisp and and the flesh is almost totally cooked through, then turn over and cook for a further 20 seconds. Remove from the pan.

6 To serve, place the roasted tomatoes in the middle of the plates. Place the fish on them and put the fennel salad on the fish. Drizzle with dressing and garnish with fennel fronds.

Gazpacho shots with tiger prawns

Dhruv Baker Ⓜ champion

Preparation time 25 minutes   **Cooking time** 2–3 minutes   **Makes 30 shots**

Ingredients

30 raw whole tiger prawns, peeled but tails left intact

salt and freshly ground black pepper

For the gazpacho

15g (½oz) fresh breadcrumbs

1 egg yolk

1 small garlic clove, crushed

3 tbsp olive oil

1 tbsp tarragon vinegar, plus extra to season, if required

1 small onion, chopped

½ red pepper, deseeded and chopped

¼ small cucumber, chopped

½ red chilli, chopped

3 tomatoes, approx. 225g (8oz), chopped

230g can plum tomatoes

1 tsp tomato purée

Method →

Method

1 To make the gazpacho, mix the breadcrumbs with the egg yolk and the garlic in a bowl, then slowly add the olive oil, mixing as you do so. Transfer to a hand-held blender or food processor and add all the remaining gazpacho ingredients. Blitz until smooth.

2 Press the mixture through a fine sieve. Taste and adjust the seasoning with salt, pepper, and vinegar if necessary. Leave to chill for at least 2 hours or overnight.

3 Have ready a large bowl of iced water. Bring a pan of water to the boil, add a pinch of salt and the peeled prawns, and cook quickly at a rolling boil for 2–3 minutes, until they just change colour. Drain and plunge into the iced water. Swish them around a bit to cool, then drain again and set aside.

4 Pour the gazpacho carefully into large, chilled shot glasses and top each one with a prawn.

How to deseed and chop peppers

Place the pepper on its side and cut off the top and bottom. Stand on one of the cut ends and slice in half lengthways. Remove the core and seeds. Open each section and lay them flat on the cutting board.

Using a sideways motion, remove any of the remaining pale, fleshy ribs. Cut the peppers into smaller sections, following the divisions of the pepper. Chop as required for the preparation of your dish.

Pea and mint soup with prosciutto

Justin Ryan @ Celebrity contestant

Preparation time 10 minutes **Cooking time** 15 minutes **Serves 4**

Ingredients

1 tbsp olive oil

2 slices of prosciutto

600ml (1 pint) chicken stock

8 sprigs of mint, leaves only

450g (1lb) frozen peas

100ml (3½fl oz) crème fraîche

salt and freshly ground black pepper

Method

1 Heat the oil in a large saucepan and fry the prosciutto until crisp. Remove from the pan and drain off excess fat on kitchen paper, then crumble into small pieces and set aside until needed. Wipe the pan out with kitchen paper.

2 Heat the stock in the wiped-out pan and add the mint and peas. Cover and boil for 5 minutes then drain, reserving the stock.

3 Transfer the peas, mint, and half the stock to a food processor. Add 60ml (2fl oz) crème fraîche and blend to a smooth paste, gradually adding the remaining stock through the funnel of the processor. Return to the pan, adding a little more stock if you prefer a thinner soup. Season to taste. Reheat but do not boil.

4 To serve, pour the soup into warm soup bowls, and garnish with a swirl of the remaining crème fraîche and the reserved pieces of prosciutto.

Crispy squid with green peppercorn and chilli dressing

Susie Carter @ quarter-finalist

Preparation time 15 minutes   **Cooking time** 5 minutes   **Serves 4**

Ingredients

4 medium squid, cleaned

juice of 1 lime

salt and freshly ground black pepper

groundnut oil, for deep-frying

3 tbsp cornflour

For the dressing

2 tbsp fresh green peppercorns

1 red chilli, deseeded and finely chopped

3cm (1¼in) piece fresh root ginger, finely grated

2 garlic cloves, crushed

3 tbsp nam pla (Thai fish sauce)

3 tbsp rice vinegar

75g (2½oz) caster sugar

2 tsp soy sauce

juice of 1 lime

To serve

4 slices of lime

coriander leaves

Method →

Method

1 To make the dressing, put all the ingredients in a small pan and simmer, stirring, until the sugar has dissolved and the mixture has thickened. Leave to cool.

2 Open out the body sacs of the squid and cut each one into about 8 rectangles. With the inside facing up, score a diamond pattern with a sharp knife, taking care not to cut all the way through. Douse with lime juice, season well with salt and pepper, and leave to cure for 2 minutes.

TECHNIQUE

How to clean squid

1 First pull the mantle (the body) and tentacles apart. The head, viscera, and ink sac will come away with the tentacles. The black "ink" can be used to flavour and colour sauces, pasta, and rice.

2 Next, push a forefinger into the body cavity, to extract the transparent, plastic-like quill (the inner lining). Hook your finger around it, pull it out and discard.

3 Heat plenty of groundnut oil in a large saucepan or deep-fat fryer to 180°C (350°F).

4 Dry the squid thoroughly on kitchen paper, then toss with the cornflour. Shake off the excess and deep fry in batches for 2 minutes until golden and crisp. Drain on kitchen paper, then quickly toss with a few spoonfuls of the dressing and serve immediately with a slice of lime on the side and coriander to garnish.

3 Separate the tentacles from the head, cutting above the eye. Discard the head and viscera, but retain the ink sac if required by your chosen recipe. (Be sure to use it immediately though, or discard.)

4 Open the tentacles to pull out the ball-shaped beak and discard it. Rinse the tentacles and mantle under cold running water, then pat dry with kitchen paper. The squid is ready to be cooked.

Seared tuna with an Asian glaze

Angela Kenny @ quarter-finalist

Preparation time 20 minutes   **Cooking time** 8 minutes   **Serves 4**

Ingredients

4 carrots

4 courgettes

8 tbsp dark soy sauce

4 limes

6 tbsp demerara sugar

12–16 Charlotte potatoes, peeled and sliced into discs

60ml (2fl oz) white miso paste

60ml (2fl oz) mirin

90ml (3½ fl oz) dry sake

2 tbsp rice wine vinegar

4 tuna steaks, 175–200g (6–7oz) each

salt and freshly ground black pepper

1 tbsp oil

Method →

Method

1 With a potato peeler, shave the carrots and courgettes into long strips. Place in a mixing bowl with 3 tbsp soy sauce, the juice and zest of 1½ limes, and 4 tbsp sugar.

2 Put the potatoes in a large pan with boiling water to cover and the white miso paste. Cook for about 10 minutes until the potatoes are tender and then drain.

3 Place the mirin, sake, remaining sugar and soy sauce, rice wine vinegar, and the juice and zest of the remaining limes in a frying pan over medium heat and reduce to a syrup consistency – about 10 minutes.

4 Season the tuna with salt and pepper. Heat the oil in another frying pan until hot, add the tuna and sear on both sides for about 3 minutes.

5 Once the tuna is cooked, transfer it to the frying pan containing the glaze and turn to coat it. Heat the ribbon vegetables in the glaze for 2 minutes, then serve with the tuna and potatoes.

Tea-smoked duck breast on egg noodles

Mark Rigby @ quarter-finalist

Preparation time 10 minutes   **Cooking time** 20 minutes   **Serves 4**

Ingredients

115g (4oz) loose jasmine tea

115g (4oz) long-grain rice

115g (4oz) dark soft brown sugar

4 duck breasts, skinned and fat removed

2 heads of pak choi, halved

500g (1lb 2oz) fresh medium egg noodles

splash of ketjap manis

splash of sesame oil

Method

1 Place the tea, rice, and sugar in a small bowl and mix together. Cut a 30cm (12in) disc of foil and place it in the bottom of a wok. Empty the mixture onto the foil and heat with the lid on over medium heat until it starts to smoke – about 5 minutes. Remove the lid and place a wire trivet over the smoking mixture. Place the duck breasts on the trivet, replace the lid, and smoke for 12–16 minutes until cooked.

2 Place the pak choi in a steamer and set over boiling water in a second wok. Cover and steam until tender – about 4–5 minutes.

3 Remove the duck from the wok and leave to rest for a few minutes. Stir-fry the noodles in a pan for 2–3 minutes, then drizzle with the ketjap manis and sesame oil and toss to combine. To serve, slice the duck breasts and place on a bed of noodles, accompanied by the pak choi.

Sang choy bao chicken wraps

Colin McAllister @ Celebrity contestant

Preparation time 20 minutes   **Cooking time** 5 minutes   **Serves 4**

Ingredients

250g (9oz) boneless, skinless chicken breast or thighs, roughly chopped

1 tsp cornflour

1 tsp soy sauce

1 tbsp vegetable oil

1 onion, finely chopped

50g (1¾oz) Chinese sausage, cut into 5mm (¼in) pieces

2 garlic cloves, finely chopped

1 tbsp sugar

pinch of salt

1 egg, lightly beaten

4 tbsp finely snipped yellow or green chives, plus whole ones to garnish

1 tbsp finely chopped coriander

1 tbsp chopped pickled ginger

6 iceberg lettuce leaves, torn in half

hoisin sauce, for dipping

Method →

Method

1 Place the chicken, cornflour, and soy sauce in a food processor and pulse until the chicken is roughly minced. Leave to stand for 10 minutes.

2 Heat a wok or large frying pan over high heat until hot. Add the oil and swirl to coat the sides.

3 Add the onion, Chinese sausage, and garlic, and cook, stirring, for about 30 seconds until fragrant.

4 Add the chicken to the wok and stir-fry until it is no longer pink but still moist – about 3 minutes.

TECHNIQUE

How to finely chop onions

1 Using a sharp chef's knife, hold the onion firmly in one hand, then cut the bulb lengthways in half and peel off the skin, leaving the root intact to hold the layers together.

2 Lay one half cut-side down on the board. Hold it in place while you make a few slices into the onion horizontally, making sure that you cut up to, but not through, the root.

5 Scatter in the sugar and salt, drizzle the egg over the chicken, and cook, stirring, for about 2 minutes until both the egg and chicken are cooked through.

6 Stir in the chives, coriander, and pickled ginger and cook for a further 30 seconds, then remove the wok from the heat.

7 To serve, spoon some of the chicken onto each halved lettuce leaf. Arrange 3 on each plate, and garnish with whole chives. To finish, place tiny dishes of hoisin sauce alongside. Roll the lettuce around the chicken, dip in the sauce, and eat straight away, while the chicken is still warm.

3 Hold the horizontally sliced onion firmly, then with the tip of your knife, slice down through the layers vertically, cutting as close to the root as possible. Repeat, slicing at regular intervals.

4 Now, cut across the vertical slices that you have just made, to produce even dice. Use the root to hold the onion steady, then discard this part when the rest of the onion has been diced.

Elderflower sorbet with marinated berries

James Shepherd @ quarter-finalist

Preparation time 20minutes **Cooking time** 5minutes **Serves 4**

Ingredients

For the sorbet

150g (5½oz) caster sugar

360ml (12fl oz) elderflower cordial

For the berries

75ml (2½ fl oz) Riesling

2 tbsp crème de cassis

juice of 1 lime

25g (scant 1oz) icing sugar

5 or 6 mint leaves, chopped

300g (10oz) mixed berries, such as strawberries, raspberries, and blueberries

Method

1 To make the sorbet, dissolve the sugar in 360ml (12fl oz) water in a saucepan on a medium heat. Increase the temperature and let the syrup boil for 5 minutes to thicken. Add the elderflower cordial and remove from the heat and leave to cool.

2 Pour the syrup into an ice-cream machine and churn for about 20 minutes, or until set. Transfer to a shallow freezer container and place in the freezer until ready to use.

3 For the berry marinade, combine the Riesling, crème de cassis, and lime juice in a bowl. Add the icing sugar, taste and add more if required – you are looking for a balance of sweet and sharp flavours. Add most of the mint leaves and set aside for the flavours to infuse.

4 To serve, wash the berries and drain them in a colander lined with kitchen paper to absorb excess water. Combine with the marinade and spoon into 4 glasses. Top with a quenelle of sorbet and decorate with the remaining mint leaves.

Summer fruit compote with scented cream

Helen Gilmour @ quarter-finalist

Preparation time 10 minutes   **Cooking time** 15 minutes   **Serves 4**

Ingredients

1 punnet each of blueberries, raspberries, strawberries, blackberries, totalling about 675g (1½ lb)

1–2 tbsp caster sugar

1½–2 tbsp rosewater

2 tbsp Greek-style yogurt

250g (9oz) mascarpone cheese

Method

1 Preheat the oven to 190°C (375°F/Gas 5).

2 Place the berries in a baking dish. Sprinkle with caster sugar to taste and bake in the oven for 10 minutes, or 15 minutes if they are taken straight from the fridge – the berries should just be beginning to ooze their juice. Remove from the oven, chill the berries over iced water, and place in the fridge to cool.

3 In a small bowl, mix the rosewater and 2 tsp sugar to dissolve the sugar. In a separate bowl, mix the yogurt with the mascarpone. Mix the rosewater and sugar with the mascarpone, adding it slowly to avoid it splitting.

4 Serve the berries in large wine glasses, topped with a good spoonful of the scented cream.

Chilli-spiced chocolate fondant

Dhruv Baker @ Celebrity semi-finalist

Preparation time 20 minutes   **Cooking time** 10 minutes   **Serves 6**

Ingredients

85g (3oz) dark chocolate (70% cocoa), broken into pieces

85g (3oz) unsalted butter, cubed, plus a little extra for greasing

2 eggs

85g (3oz) caster sugar

½ red chilli, deseeded and finely diced

30g (1oz) plain flour

2 tbsp cocoa powder

¼ tsp cayenne pepper

icing sugar for dusting

2 red chillies, deseeded and sliced, to decorate

Method

Method

1 Preheat the oven to 200°C (400°F/Gas 6) and grease 6 dariole moulds. Place the chocolate and butter in a bain-marie or a bowl set over a pan of simmering water, making sure that the base of the bowl is clear of the water. When the chocolate and butter have melted and combined, remove from the heat and leave to stand for 5 minutes.

2 Using an electric whisk, beat together the eggs and sugar in a bowl until thick and pale. Slowly whisk in the chocolate and butter mixture. When it is well incorporated, fold in the chilli. Sift the flour, cocoa powder, and cayenne pepper over and fold in gently with a metal spoon.

3 Divide the mixture between the dariole moulds, place in the oven and cook for 10 minutes until firm on top and starting to come away from the sides of the moulds. Remove and leave to stand for 2 minutes, before loosening the edges and turning out onto the plates. Dust with the icing sugar and lay some slices of chilli on the plates to decorate, before serving.

How to deseed and cut chillies

Cut the chilli lengthways in half. Using the tip of your knife, scrape out the seeds and remove the membrane and stem. Turn the chilli half flesh-side down and flatten with the palm of your hand. Turn it over again and slice it lengthways into strips. For dice, hold the strips of cut chillies firmly together and carefully slice crossways to make equal-size pieces.

45 Minutes and Under

Warm Roquefort cheesecake with oven-roasted tomatoes

James Shepherd @ quarter-finalist

Preparation time 20 minutes   **Cooking time** 30 minutes   **Serves 4**

Ingredients

For the cheesecake base

85g (3oz) fresh white bread

45g (1½oz) unsalted butter

salt and freshly ground black pepper

For the cheesecake filling

100g (3½oz) full-fat cream cheese

75g (2½oz) Roquefort cheese

1 large egg, yolk only

1 tsp cornflour

1 tbsp double cream

squeeze of lemon juice

For the roasted tomatoes

20 cherry tomatoes on the vine

olive oil, for roasting

For the basil oil

30g (1oz) basil

75ml (2½fl oz) olive oil

Method

Method

1 Preheat the oven to 190°C (375°F/Gas 5). Butter the bases and sides of four 8cm (3in) fluted, loose-bottomed flan tins.

2 For the cheesecake base, put the bread in a food processor and whizz until it has turned into fine crumbs. Melt the butter over a gentle heat in a saucepan, tip in the breadcrumbs, season, and stir to combine. Press the mixture into the bottom and sides of the flan tins, pressing down with the back of a spoon to ensure an even layer. Bake in the oven for about 10 minutes or until the base is golden – keep watch as it can overcook very quickly. Keep the oven on for roasting the tomatoes.

3 For the filling, cream together all the ingredients and divide between the flan tins. Return to the oven and bake for 10–12 minutes or until golden and just set (there should be a slight wobble when you shake the tins). Remove the cheesecakes from the oven and allow them to cool slightly before removing from the tins.

4 Split the tomato vine so there are 5 tomatoes per person. Place them on a baking tray, drizzle over some olive oil and roast in the oven for about 10 minutes or until the skins start to blister.

5 Meanwhile, make the basil oil. Blanch the basil leaves in salted boiling water and then refresh in cold water. Place in a blender with the olive oil and pulse until the liquid is moving freely, adding more oil if necessary. Pour into a muslin-lined sieve over a bowl to drain. Decant the oil into a jug.

6 To serve, place each cheesecake on a plate, top with the cherry tomatoes, and add a drizzle of basil oil.

Curried butternut squash soup

Michelle Peters @ semi-finalist

Preparation time 15 minutes   **Cooking time** 30 minutes   **Serves 4**

Ingredients

15g (½oz) unsalted butter

1 onion, chopped

1cm (½in) piece of fresh root ginger, finely chopped

4 garlic cloves, finely chopped

2 tsp ground coriander

1 tsp ground cumin

2 tsp garam masala

1½ tsp hot chilli powder

1 butternut squash, peeled, deseeded, and cut into large chunks

500ml (16fl oz) vegetable stock

salt and freshly ground black pepper

200ml (7fl oz) coconut milk

2 tbsp coconut cream

2 tbsp chopped fresh coriander

Method

1 Melt the butter in a large pan and sauté the onion for about 3 minutes with the ginger and garlic.

2 Add the spices to the onion mixture and fry for 5–7 minutes to develop their flavour.

3 Add the butternut squash to the pan with the stock. Season. Bring to the boil, then simmer for about 20 minutes until the squash is tender. Add the coconut milk and stir.

4 Blitz with a hand blender or transfer to a food processor and blend until a smooth consistency is reached.

5 Ladle the soup into 4 bowls. Serve with a dash of coconut cream, fresh coriander, and a sprinkle of freshly ground black pepper.

Smoked haddock timbale with poached quail's egg

Christine Hamilton @ Celebrity finalist

Preparation time 15 minutes   **Cooking time** 30 minutes   **Serves 4**

Ingredients

4 baby beetroots (or
1 mature beetroot,
peeled and quartered)

salt and freshly ground
black pepper

splash of olive oil

2–3 sprigs of thyme
(optional)

butter for greasing

150g (5½oz) smoked
haddock fillet, skin
removed

400ml (14fl oz) double
cream

4 egg yolks

2 tbsp chopped dill

2 tbsp chopped chives

4 quail's eggs

For the salad dressing

1 tbsp lemon juice

½ tbsp olive oil

½ tbsp walnut oil

½ tbsp wholegrain
mustard

1 tbsp caster sugar

ground black pepper

To serve

small bag of rocket
and watercress

50g (1¾oz) walnut
pieces

Method →

Method

1 Preheat the oven to 170°C (340°F/Gas 3–4). Season the beetroots with salt and pepper and wrap tightly in kitchen foil with olive oil and thyme (if using). Roast in a corner of the oven for 30 minutes.

2 Butter 4 timbale moulds. Poach the haddock lightly for 2–3 minutes in 200ml (7fl oz) of cream. Drain and reserve the cream.

3 In a bowl, whisk together the reserved and remaining cream, egg yolks, dill, chives, and a good pinch of black pepper.

4 Break the haddock into pieces with a fork and divide between the timbale moulds. Pour the cream mixture into each mould.

5 Place the moulds in a deep roasting tray or oven dish. Add 3–4cm (1¼ –1½in) of water to the tray or dish before placing it in the preheated oven on a high shelf. Bake for 20 minutes, or until the timbales are set and do not wobble when moved.

6 Meanwhile, poach the quail's eggs by breaking each gently into a pan of gently simmering water and poaching for 30 seconds. When cooked, plunge into iced water.

7 In a small bowl, whisk together all the ingredients for the lemon and walnut dressing.

8 Remove the timbales from the oven and allow to cool before unmoulding. Arrange dressed salad leaves on each plate, with diced beetroot, and sprinkle over finely chopped walnut pieces. Position a timbale in the centre and place a poached quail's egg on top.

How to poach eggs

Carefully crack an egg onto a small plate, then slide it into a pan of gently simmering water mixed with a drop of vinegar. With a slotted spoon, gently lift the white over the yolk until set.

Poach for 3–5 minutes (or a medium hen's egg). Before serving, place the egg in another pan of just-simmering salted water for 30 seconds to remove the taste of the vinegar.

Hake with salsa verde and crushed new potatoes

Aggie MacKenzie @ Celebrity semi-finalist

Preparation time 20 minutes   **Cooking time** 20 minutes   **Serves 4**

Ingredients

For the potatoes

400g (14oz) small new potatoes

1 tbsp extra virgin olive oil

1 bunch of spring onions, finely sliced

1 tbsp parsley, chopped

salt and freshly ground black pepper

For the salsa verde

20g (¾oz) parsley, chopped

20g (¾oz) basil, chopped

20g (¾oz) mint, chopped

3 canned anchovies, drained and chopped

1 tbsp Dijon mustard

100ml (3½fl oz) extra virgin olive oil

2 tbsp red wine vinegar

1 garlic clove, finely chopped

For the fish

4 hake fillets, each weighing approx. 175g (6oz)

seasoned flour, to dredge

1 tbsp groundnut oil

25g (scant 1oz) butter

To serve

lemon wedges

Method

1 Boil the potatoes in a large pan of salted water until tender. Drain, roughly crush, then add the olive oil, spring onions, and parsley. Season to taste and toss gently.

2 Meanwhile, mix together the ingredients for the salsa verde, season to taste, then set aside.

3 Toss the fish in the seasoned flour, then shake off any excess.

4 Heat the groundnut oil in a frying pan, then add the fish, skin-side down, and fry for 3–4 minutes until the skin is crisp. Turn over the fish, add the butter, and cook for a further 2 minutes, basting the fish with the butter continuously.

5 Remove fish from the pan and drain on kitchen paper.

6 To serve, place the fish on plates with the salsa verde spooned over, and the crushed potatoes to one side. Serve with lemon wedges to squeeze over the fish.

Potato soup with parsley pesto

Julia Paterson @ quarter-finalist

Preparation time 15 minutes   **Cooking time** 30 minutes   **Serves 4**

Ingredients

½ tbsp olive oil

2 rashers smoked back bacon, chopped

225g (8oz) onions, chopped

225g (8oz) floury potatoes, such as Maris Piper or King Edwards

300ml (10fl oz) chicken stock

300ml (10fl oz) milk

25g (scant 1oz) conchigliette pasta

For the pesto

75g (2½oz) flat-leaf parsley

2 garlic cloves

60g (2oz) pine nuts

60g (2oz) Parmesan cheese, freshly grated

white pepper

2 tbsp olive oil

To serve

300ml (10fl oz) double cream

chopped flat-leaf parsley

Parmesan cheese shavings

Method

1 Heat the oil in a large saucepan. Sauté the bacon for about 5 minutes, stirring occasionally, until starting to brown. Add the onion and cook for a further 5 minutes until softened and translucent.

2 Meanwhile, peel and dice the potatoes. Add to the pan with the stock and milk and simmer for 8 minutes. Add the pasta and simmer for a further 10 minutes until soft.

3 Put all the pesto ingredients into a blender or food processor and blitz until a smooth consistency is reached.

4 To serve, add the cream to the soup, bring it back to the boil, and ladle into bowls. Serve hot with a sprinkling of parsley, a swirl of pesto, and a few Parmesan shavings.

Smoked haddock risotto with a poached hen's egg

Alice Cooper @ quarter-finalist

Preparation time 10 minutes   **Cooking time** 30 minutes   **Serves 4**

Ingredients

1 tbsp olive oil

60g (2oz) salted butter

1 onion, finely chopped

1 celery stick, finely chopped

200g (7oz) arborio rice

150ml (5fl oz) white wine

1 litre (1¾ pints) simmering chicken stock

150g (5½oz) fillet of undyed smoked haddock, chopped

50g (1¾ oz) baby leaf spinach

grated zest and juice of 1 lemon

50g (1¾oz) Parmesan cheese, freshly grated

salt and freshly ground black pepper

3 tbsp white wine vinegar

4 eggs

Method

1 Heat the oil and half the butter in a large saucepan. Add the onion and celery and fry on medium heat until soft. Add the rice, cook for a few minutes, and then add the wine. Once the wine has been absorbed, start adding the simmering stock, bit by bit, allowing the rice to absorb all the liquid before adding more.

2 Once the rice is nearly cooked, after about 20 minutes, add the haddock, spinach, and lemon zest. Then, once the rice is done, stir in the lemon juice, Parmesan cheese, and the rest of the butter, and adjust the seasoning. Place a lid on the pan, remove from the heat, and leave to rest for 5 minutes while you cook the eggs.

TECHNIQUE

How to make risotto

1 Heat 900ml (1½ pints) stock to a simmer in a pan. In another, wide-based pan, heat 1 tbsp olive oil and 75g (2½oz) butter. Stir in 300g (10oz) risotto rice, coating the grains in the butter and oil.

2 Add 75ml (2½fl oz) white wine and boil, stirring until absorbed. Then add a ladle of simmering stock and stir until absorbed. Continue adding hot stock, a ladle at at time, and stirring constantly.

3 To poach each egg, bring a saucepan of water to the boil and add the vinegar. Create a whirlpool and crack the egg into the centre. Reduce the heat and simmer for 4 minutes or until the white has set. If not using straight away, then place in ice-cold water to arrest the cooking process, so keeping a soft yolk.

4 To serve, spoon out the risotto into a neat round on a plate, using a ring mould if necessary. Top with the poached egg.

3 Continue adding the stock and stirring with a wooden spoon until the rice is tender, but retains a slight bite. Add a knob of butter, season with salt and pepper to taste, and take off the heat.

4 The constant stirring releases the starch in the rice, so the risotto should now have a creamy texture. Cover the pan and leave the risotto to rest for several minutes before serving.

Fresh sardines with pine nuts and anchovies

Linda Lusardi @ Celebrity semi-finalist

Preparation time 15 minutes   **Cooking time** 30 minutes   **Serves 4**

Ingredients

40g (1¼oz) sultanas

5 tbsp olive oil, plus extra for greasing

250g (9oz) fresh white breadcrumbs

40g (1¼oz) pine nuts

2 tbsp chopped parsley

40g can anchovies, drained and chopped

pinch of freshly grated nutmeg

salt and freshly ground black pepper

12 fresh sardines, scaled, gutted, and heads and back bones removed

12 bay leaves

4 tbsp lemon juice

2 large potatoes

15g (½oz) butter

4 large carrots, sliced

lemon wedges, to garnish

Method →

Method

1 Preheat the oven to 180°C (350°F/Gas 4). Put the sultanas in a small bowl and cover with boiling water. Leave them to soak for 10 minutes, then drain.

2 Heat the oil in a frying pan. Add half the breadcrumbs and fry over medium heat, turning them frequently, until golden brown.

3 Remove from the heat and add the sultanas, pine nuts, 1 tbsp of the parsley, the anchovies, nutmeg, salt, and pepper.

4 Place a little of the mixture inside each sardine and press the sides together to close. Brush a large ovenproof dish with olive oil. Arrange the sardines side by side in a single layer in the dish. Place a bay leaf between each fish.

5 Sprinkle the remaining breadcrumbs over the top, drizzle with a little extra olive oil, and bake in the oven for 20 minutes. Sprinkle with the lemon juice before serving.

6 Meanwhile, boil the potatoes in a large pan of salted water until soft. Drain and mash with the butter and remaining parsley.

7 Boil the carrots in a separate pan of salted water for about 10 minutes, or until tender, then drain.

8 Serve the sardines with the mashed potatoes, carrots, and garnished with lemon wedges.

Sorrel soup with egg

inspired by **Marta Perepeczko-Foley** @ quarter-finalist
Preparation time 20 minutes   **Cooking time** 25 minutes   **Serves 4**

Ingredients

60g (2oz) butter
1 onion, chopped
1 large potato, peeled and diced
300g (10oz) sorrel
1 litre (1¾ pints) chicken stock

salt and freshly ground black pepper
4 tbsp double cream
2 tbsp white wine vinegar
4 eggs

Method

1 Melt the butter in a saucepan and gently fry the onion for about 10 minutes until softened but not browned. Add the potato and half of the sorrel leaves to the pan and stir well, then cook for a further 2–3 minutes, covered.

2 Pour in the chicken stock and bring to the boil, then simmer for about 10–15 minutes or until the potato is tender. Remove from the heat, stir in the remaining sorrel leaves, and process until smooth using a hand blender. Season well with salt and pepper and stir in 3 tbsp of the cream. Cook on a gentle heat for about 2 minutes, until steaming (do not boil or the bright green colour will be lost).

3 In a separate pan, bring some water to the boil and add the vinegar. Crack each egg into a cup. Swirl the water round, then carefully tip each egg into the water and poach for 2–3 minutes. Remove with a slotted spoon to drain on kitchen paper.

4 Serve soup in warmed bowls. Place a poached egg in the centre of each and garnish with the remaining drizzle of cream.

Red mullet with purple sprouting broccoli and courgette gratin

Christopher Souto @ semi-finalist

Preparation time 35 minutes   **Cooking time** 10–15 minutes   **Serves 4**

Ingredients

16–20 medium Charlotte potatoes, peeled

salt and freshly ground black pepper

125g (4½oz) clarified butter

4 medium red mullet, filleted, skin on, or 4 pink trout fillets

For the gratins

400g (14oz) medium-sized courgettes

400g (14oz) purple sprouting broccoli florets

25g (scant 1oz) clarified butter

good pinch of paprika

2 tbsp double cream

good pinch of grated nutmeg

For the sauce

75 ml (2½fl oz) white wine

1 tbsp white wine vinegar

2 tbsp Noilly Prat or other dry vermouth

75g (2½oz) butter

To garnish

½ tsp salmon caviar

4 chervil or flat-leaf parsley leaves

Method →

Method

1 Cut the potatoes to an even barrel shape. Parboil in salted water for about 7–8 minutes, then drain and dry off. Melt 100g (3½oz) clarified butter in a medium-sized frying pan. Cook the potatoes for about 8–10 minutes until evenly browned and crisp on the outside and soft inside. Keep warm.

2 For the gratins, finely slice half the courgettes lengthways, using a mandolin or potato peeler. Blanch them for 30 seconds in salted boiling water and refresh in iced water. Drain well and set aside.

3 Chop the purple sprouting broccoli florets and leaves into smallish pieces. Discard any slightly thick stems. Melt the clarified butter in a frying pan or wok and stir-fry the broccoli for 2 minutes, stirring constantly. Sprinkle with

TECHNIQUE

How to prepare courgettes

1 Place the courgette on a board and cut off both ends. Cut it in half lengthways, then hold the courgette firmly on its side and cut each half again to make slices 5mm (¼ in) thick.

2 Put each slice of courgette flat on the board and cut across it with a sharp knife to make equal-sized batonettes, or sticks. To make dice, simply line up the batonettes and cut across them.

2–3 tbsp hot water and continue to stir for another 1–2 minutes until the broccoli is tender and wilted down. Remove from the heat and season well with the paprika, salt, and pepper. Set aside.

4 Peel and dice the remaining courgettes. Blend with the double cream and season generously with pepper and grated nutmeg. Set aside.

5 Preheat the grill to very hot. To assemble the gratins, butter four 7cm (2¾in) metal cooking rings or ring moulds. Cut out and butter 4 squares of greaseproof paper, a little larger than the cooking rings. Lay them on a baking sheet and put the cooking rings on top. Line the base and sides of the rings with the blanched courgette slices, ensuring there are no gaps. Layer them with the purple sprouting broccoli, pressing the mixture down well into the rings. Cover with the puréed courgette, filling the cooking ring to the top. Smooth over. Cook the gratins under a hot grill for about 7–8 minutes until hot, and the puréed courgette has just started to colour.

6 To make the sauce, put the wine, vinegar and Noilly Prat in a saucepan and reduce by two-thirds. Gradually whisk in the butter until smooth and glossy. Keep warm.

Method

7 Melt the remaining 25g (scant 1oz) clarified butter and use to brush the fish fillets. Season and pan-fry over a medium-high heat, skin-side down, for about 3 minutes or until the fish just begins to turn opaque.

8 To serve, put the butter-sautéed potatoes on 4 warmed serving plates and place the fish fillets on top. Carefully invert the vegetable gratins onto the plates and garnish with the salmon caviar. Drizzle the vermouth butter sauce over the fish and garnish with chervil or parsley.

How to pan-fry fish fillets

TECHNIQUE

1 Heat equal amounts of oil and butter in a heavy frying pan over a medium-high heat until foaming. Season the fish, then add it to the pan, skin-side down, and fry for half the time specified in your recipe.

2 Use a spatula or fish slice to turn the pieces over, then continue frying the fish for the remaining cooking time, or until it is light golden brown and the flesh flakes easily when tested with a fork.

Indonesian noodle soup

Simon Spindley @ quarter-finalist

Preparation time 30 minutes   **Cooking time** 10 minutes   **Serves 4**

Ingredients

1 litre (1¾ pints) clear chicken stock

2 tbsp mirin (Japanese rice wine)

2 tbsp nam pla (Thai fish sauce)

1 garlic clove, finely chopped

2 tbsp white wine vinegar

1 small fresh red chilli, deseeded and finely diced

grated zest and juice of 1 lime

1 small chicken breast fillet, finely diced

2 tbsp white sugar

2 tbsp dark soy sauce

2 tbsp Worcestershire sauce

3 spring onions, finely diced

1 head of pak choi, finely diced

1 red pepper, deseeded and finely diced

30g (1oz) fine dried rice noodles

50g (1¾oz) fine green beans, diced

300g (10oz) chestnut mushrooms, diced

sprigs of coriander

Method

1 Put the stock, mirin, nam pla, garlic, vinegar, chilli, and lime juice and zest in a large pan. Bring to the boil, then turn down the heat and simmer for 10 minutes.

2 Add the chicken and return to the boil, then simmer for 10 minutes. After checking the taste, add the sugar, dark soy sauce, and Worcestershire sauce.

3 Add the spring onions, pak choi, and red pepper to the pan. Add the noodles to the pan with the remaining diced ingredients and cook for 3 minutes before serving. Garnish with coriander leaves and serve with boiled rice as an accompaniment.

Pan-fried fillet of pike with crayfish, wilted sorrel, and watercress sauce

Tom Whitaker @ finalist

Preparation time 20 minutes   **Cooking time** 30 minutes   **Serves 4**

Ingredients

For the sauce

3 bay leaves

10 peppercorns

12 freshwater crayfish, chilled for 2 hours in the freezer

250ml (8fl oz) double cream

300g (10oz) watercress, hard stalks removed

1 tsp English mustard powder

For the pike

2 tbsp rapeseed oil

4 pike fillets, 100g (3½oz) each, pin-boned and with skin on

To serve

250g (9oz) sorrel leaves, thoroughly washed

Method

1 Bring a pan of water, just big enough to hold the crayfish, to the boil with the bay leaves and peppercorns. Add the chilled crayfish and boil for 5 minutes. Lift out of the pan with a slotted spoon. When cool enough to handle, remove the heads and claws and peel the tails, reserving the meat. Return heads, claws, and tail shells to the pan and simmer for 30 minutes to reduce liquid. Strain the liquid into a clean pan and add the cream. Bring to the boil and reduce by a third.

Method →

Method

2 Add the watercress and mustard powder to the sauce, return to the boil, and simmer for 2 minutes. Remove the bay leaves, place sauce in a jug blender, and blitz until smooth, then pour into a pan and keep warm until needed.

3 For the pike, preheat the oven to 200°C (400°F/Gas 6). Heat the oil in a frying pan over medium to high heat. Once it is hot, add the pike fillets skin-side down and cook them for 3–5 minutes until the skin is golden. Flip the fish and brown lightly again. Remove the fish to a roasting tray and place in the oven for 6–8 minutes, or until just cooked through.

4 To serve, divide sorrel leaves between 4 bowls. Top with hot pike fillets and 3 crayfish tails. Spoon hot sauce over and serve immediately.

TECHNIQUE

How to deshell crayfish

1 Crayfish should be cooked in a large pan of boiling water or flavoured broth for 5–7 minutes and then removed to cool. When cool enough to handle, simply break off head section and claws.

2 Now hold the tail between your thumb and forefinger, and gently squeeze the tail until you hear the shell crack. Remove the meat in one piece by carefully pulling away the sides of the shell.

Cauliflower and barberry fritters with yogurt sauce

Mitra Abrahams @ semi-finalist

Preparation time 20minutes   **Cooking time** 15minutes   **Serves 4**

Ingredients

For the yogurt sauce

150g (5½oz) Greek yogurt

2 tsp chopped coriander

zest and juice of ½ lime

dash of olive oil

salt and freshly ground black pepper

For the fritters

1 small cauliflower, about 125g (4½oz), cut into small florets

60g (2oz) plain flour

1 tsp ground cumin

½ tsp ground cinnamon

½ tsp ground turmeric

2 large eggs, beaten

1 shallot, finely chopped

½ garlic clove, finely chopped

2 tbsp parsley, plus extra to garnish

30g (1oz) dried barberries, available from Iranian shops as zereshk

groundnut oil, for deep frying

Method

1 For the sauce, place the yogurt, coriander, lime zest and juice, and olive oil into a small bowl. Season and mix together.

2 For the fritters, place the cauliflower in a pan of boiling salted water and simmer for 3–4 minutes or until just tender. Drain, then refresh under cold water to stop the cauliflower cooking further. Set aside.

3 Mix the flour and spices together in a bowl. Make a well in the middle, add the egg, and beat with a whisk until smooth. Add the shallot, garlic, parsley, barberries, cooked cauliflower, and a sprinkling of salt and pepper, and mix well.

4 Heat the oil in a deep pan to 190ºC (375°F) or until a cube of bread turns golden brown in 30 seconds. Carefully lower tablespoonfuls of the mixture in batches into the hot oil. Fry for 2–3 minutes or until golden brown. Remove with a slotted spoon and drain on kitchen paper. Repeat to make 12 fritters.

5 Serve 3 fritters per person, scattered with chopped parsley, with the sauce on the side.

Roast turbot with lobster and lobster cream sauce

Wendi Peters @ Celebrity finalist

Preparation time 10 minutes   **Cooking time** 45 minutes   **Serves 4**

Ingredients

1 lobster, cooked, deshelled, and sliced (keep the shells for the sauce)

4 turbot fillets, 125g (4½oz) each, skinned

2 tbsp light olive oil

25g (scant 1oz) unsalted butter

salt and freshly ground white pepper

For the cream sauce

1 tbsp light olive oil

2 tbsp chopped carrot

2 tbsp chopped onion

3 garlic cloves, crushed

1 tbsp tomato purée

2 tbsp brandy

150ml (5fl oz) white wine

300ml (10fl oz) double cream

For the vinaigrette

½ tsp Dijon mustard

1½ tbsp white wine vinegar

salt and cracked black pepper

90ml (3fl oz) extra virgin olive oil

½ tsp crushed garlic

1 tsp chopped tarragon

½ tbsp chopped flat-leaf parsley

½ tbsp snipped chives

1 plum tomato, skinned, halved, deseeded and cut into 5mm (¼in) dice

To serve

3 large King Edward potatoes, peeled and cut into chunks

20g (¾oz) butter

3 tbsp double cream, warmed

Method →

Method

1 To make the sauce, heat the oil in a very large pan until smoking. Roughly chop the lobster shells, toss into the pot and sauté over high heat for 3 minutes. Add the vegetables and garlic and cook for a further 2 minutes. Stir in the tomato purée, brandy, and wine and simmer until the wine is reduced by half. Add 600ml (1 pint) of boiling water, reduce the heat and simmer for 20 minutes. Strain through a fine sieve into a clean pan then simmer to reduce to about 250ml (8fl oz). Add the cream and boil until thick and creamy, then set aside.

2 Meanwhile, bring a large pan of salted water to the boil, add the potatoes and simmer for 20 minutes until cooked. Drain, mash, and season with salt and pepper. Add the butter and warmed cream. Keep warm.

TECHNIQUE

How to prepare lobster

1 Rinse the lobster under cold running water and pat dry with kitchen paper, then place on a cutting board. Take hold of the tail and twist it sharply away from the body to detach it.

2 Set the body aside and turn the tail over with the shell-side down. Using a pair of sharp kitchen scissors, and beginning at the far end of the tail, cut down the centre towards the thickest part.

3 To make the vinaigrette, whisk together the mustard, vinegar, and some seasoning. Whisk in the oil, then the garlic and herbs. Stir in the tomato dice. Transfer to a pan.

4 Season the turbot. Heat the oil in a large heavy frying pan until almost smoking. Add the butter and as it begins to foam put the turbot into the pan. Sauté for about 3 minutes on each side. Meanwhile, gently heat the sliced lobster in the vinaigrette.

5 To serve, put the mash on warmed plates and place the turbot on top. Spoon the lobster and vinaigrette alongside and drizzle the plates with lobster cream sauce.

3 Using your thumbs, pull the shell apart along the line where you cut it with scissors, and fold the shell back. You should now be able to extract the meat in one piece.

4 To remove the meat from the claws, crack them open with a lobster cracker or a small hammer. Once the shell is open, extract the meat inside carefully, and discard any attached membrane.

Pan-fried chicken breast with sesame seeds and a mango hollandaise

Jaye Wakelin @ quarter-finalist

Preparation time 15 minutes   **Cooking time** 20 minutes   **Serves 4**

Ingredients

4 chicken breasts, skinned

2 large egg yolks

salt and freshly ground black pepper

1 tbsp lemon juice

1 tbsp white wine vinegar

125g (4½oz) salted butter

1 ripe mango, peeled, stoned and chopped

2 tbsp sesame seeds

1 tbsp groundnut oil

25g (scant 1oz) butter

400g (14oz) purple sprouting broccoli

Method →

Method

1 Remove the chicken from the fridge at least 30 minutes before preparation.

2 To make the hollandaise, place the egg yolks in a blender with salt and pepper to taste and blend thoroughly. Heat the lemon juice and vinegar to simmering point in a small saucepan, then remove the pan from the heat. Switch on the blender again and pour the hot lemon liquid through the vent in the top of it in a steady stream. Switch off the blender.

3 In the same saucepan, melt the butter over low heat. With the blender running as before, add the butter to the egg mixture in a steady stream. The mixture should now look like runny mayonnaise. Pour it out into a clean bowl.

TECHNIQUE

How to prepare mango

1 Standing the mango on its side, cut it by running your knife just to one side of the stone; repeat the cut on the other side, so that a single slice remains with the stone encased.

2 With halves flesh-side up, cut the flesh into strips lengthways, then crossways, but not through the skin. Invert the skin to expose the flesh. Run your knife along the skin to remove the segments.

4 Add the chopped mango to the blender and blitz until smooth and puréed. Stir into the hollandaise, cover with cling film and set aside.

5 Spread the sesame seeds over a plate and press the chicken breasts onto them, coating each one evenly. Melt the oil and butter in a frying pan over medium heat, taking care that the butter doesn't brown. Add the chicken breasts and fry gently on both sides until cooked through – about 5–8 minutes on each side. At this point the butter in the pan will look brown but will not have burnt. Meanwhile, steam the broccoli until tender – about 8 minutes.

6 Return the mango hollandaise to a clean saucepan and reheat gently, taking care not to let it bubble and separate. Put the sliced chicken breasts on plates and spoon over the hollandaise. Serve with the cooked broccoli. This dish also goes well with any Chinese green, stir-fried with a little soya sauce.

How to make a traditional hollandaise

1 In a small pan, boil 2 tbsp vinegar, 2 tbsp water, and 1 tbsp of white peppercorns. Simmer for 1 minute, or until reduced by one-third.

2 Remove from the heat and leave to chill completely. Strain the liquid into a heatproof bowl, add 4 egg yolks, and whisk.

3 Place the bowl over a pan of simmering water. Whisk the mixture for 5–6 minutes, or until the sauce is thick and creamy.

4 Stand the bowl on a tea towel. Slowly pour in 250g (9oz) of clarified butter and whisk until the sauce is thick, glossy, and smooth.

5 Gently whisk in the juice of half a lemon, and season to taste with freshly ground white pepper, a pinch of cayenne pepper, and salt.

6 The hollandaise is now ready, and should be served immediately. This recipe will make 600ml (1 pint).

Warm salad of langoustines and fennel

Becky McCracken @ semi-finalist

Preparation time 30minutes   **Cooking time** 10 minutes   **Serves 4**

Ingredients

500ml (16fl oz) fish stock

16 raw langoustines or large prawns in their shells

2 tsp salted butter

2 bulbs fennel, finely sliced and the tops reserved

few sprigs of chervil, leaves chopped

few sprigs of dill, leaves chopped

Method

1 Bring the fish stock up to a slow boil in a large saucepan. Place the langoustines or prawns in the pan with the fish stock and cover with a lid. Leave to cook for 7 minutes, then take out of the stock and put to one side to cool.

2 Melt the butter in a pan on medium heat and add the sliced fennel. Soften for 3–4 minutes, until it goes slightly translucent. Take 4–6 tbsp of the langoustine broth and pour over the fennel. Set aside.

3 Meanwhile, shell the langoustines or prawns, leaving 1 per person with the shell on, as they look so pretty.

4 Mix the herbs with the langoustines (or prawns) and fennel, and arrange on the plates. Serve with a slice of ciabatta.

Lamb fillet with potatoes, carrots, and asparagus, wrapped in Parma ham

Phil Vickery MBE @ Celebrity champion

Preparation time 10 minutes   **Cooking time** 30 minutes   **Serves 4**

Ingredients

For the potatoes

600ml (1 pint) chicken stock

2 sprigs of thyme

1 bay leaf

12 small Maris Piper potatoes, trimmed to even shape

salt and freshly ground black pepper

For the lamb

2 lamb loin fillets

4 carrots, roughly chopped

2 tbsp duck fat, at room temperature

15g (½oz) butter

For the garnish

12 asparagus spears

12 baby carrots, scrubbed

few sprigs of mint, finely chopped

12 slices of Parma ham

30g (1oz) butter

For the sauce

15g (½oz) butter

1 tbsp duck fat

½ onion, finely chopped

3 tbsp Madeira

400ml (14fl oz) chicken stock

2 sprigs of thyme

2 bay leaves

Method →

Method

1 Preheat the oven to 180°C (350°F/Gas 4). For the potatoes, heat the chicken stock in a pan with herbs. Place the potatoes in a roasting tin. Pour over the hot stock, season, and roast for 10–15 minutes, basting often, until soft. Remove and set aside.

2 Season the lamb well. Place the roughly chopped carrots in a small roasting tin with 1 tbsp of the duck fat. Stir well. Roast in the oven for 10-15 minutes, while preparing the garnish. Trim 2cm (¾in) off the ends of the asparagus. Blanch with the baby carrots for 2 minutes, then refresh in iced water.

3 Sprinkle some mint on a slice of the Parma ham and roll up a spear of asparagus in the ham. Secure with a cocktail stick. Repeat with the other spears and ham. Set aside.

4 Heat the 15g (½oz) of butter and remaining 1 tbsp of duck fat in a frying pan over medium heat and sear the lamb for a minute until brown all over. Place on top of the roasting chopped carrots in the oven and roast for 7–10 minutes, according to taste. Wrap meat in foil, and keep warm.

5 For the sauce, heat the butter and duck fat in a pan, add the onion and cook until soft. Add the Madeira, and reduce by half. Add the stock, the lamb juices and roasted carrots, and herbs. Reduce by half. Strain through a sieve and check the seasoning. Reheat before serving.

6 Fry the asparagus rolls until the ham is crisp. Remove the sticks.

7 Toss the baby carrots in 15g (½oz) of hot butter in a pan. Repeat with the remaining butter and the potatoes. Season to taste.

8 Slice each lamb loin into 8 slices. Arrange on serving plates, surround with the vegetables and a drizzle of the sauce.

How to glaze carrots

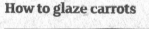

1 Put lightly cooked carrots in a hot sauté pan with about 1 tbsp each of butter and sugar (vary quantities with amount and size of carrots).

2 Turn and toss the carrots until they are tender and coated in a delicious butter and sugar glaze. Serve immediately.

Pigeon breast with apple and black pudding, and a cider jus

Phil Vickery MBE @ **Celebrity champion**

Preparation time 10 minutes   **Cooking time** 30 minutes   **Serves 4**

Ingredients

4 eating apples, ideally British Cox's, peeled and cored

2 tbsp duck fat, at room temperature

20g (¾oz) butter

salt and freshly ground black pepper

200g (7oz) black pudding, diced

4 pigeon breasts

250ml (8fl oz) dry cider

To garnish

50g (1¾oz) pea shoots

50g (1¾oz) watercress

Method

1 Preheat the oven to 180°C (350°F/Gas 4). Chop each apple into 8 pieces. Heat 1 tbsp duck fat and the butter in a frying pan over medium to high heat. Season apple with salt and pepper, add to pan, and fry for 2 minutes until golden. Remove with a slotted spoon and transfer to a non-stick baking tray. Bake for 10 minutes until just tender.

2 Fry the black pudding in the frying pan for 5–6 minutes until crisp. Drain on kitchen paper, then spread out on a baking tray and bake in the oven for 10 minutes until crisp.

3 Using the same pan, heat the remaining duck fat over high heat. Season the pigeon breasts, add them to the pan skin-side down, and sear for 1 minute. Turn over and add the cider. Cook for 2 minutes, then remove from the pan and rest on a warm plate. Boil cider until reduced by half, then remove from the heat.

4 To serve, slice pigeon breasts thinly. Place 8 pieces of the apple on each plate and then lay slices of pigeon on top. Garnish with the black pudding, pea shoots, and watercress, and finish with a drizzle of the cider jus.

Crispy butterfly prawns with ginger and lime

Perveen Nekoo @ quarter-finalist

Preparation time 30 minutes   **Cooking time** 10 minutes   **Serves 4**

Ingredients

12 large raw black tiger prawns, heads and shells removed, tails left on

juice and zest of 1½ limes

1 tsp grated fresh root ginger

½ tsp turmeric

salt

35g (1¼ oz) coriander, finely chopped

70–75g (2¼–2½oz) fresh white breadcrumbs

60g (2oz) plain flour

1 large egg, beaten

60g (2oz) salted butter

2 tbsp olive oil

lime wedges, to serve

Method

1 Devein and butterfly the prawns. In a bowl, mix the lime juice, ginger, turmeric, salt, and half the coriander. Add the prawns to this mixture and leave to marinate for 20 minutes.

2 In a separate bowl, mix the remaining coriander with the breadcrumbs and lime zest.

3 Dip the prawns in the flour, then the egg, and finally the breadcrumb mixture. Repeat the egg and breadcrumb sequence to give them a good coating.

4 Heat the butter and oil in a pan until they start to sizzle. Add the coated prawns and fry until golden. Remove and drain on kitchen paper. Serve with wedges of fresh lime.

Seared saddle of venison with a port and balsamic reduction

Becky McCracken @ semi-finalist

Preparation time 15 minutes   **Cooking time** 35 minutes   **Serves 4**

Ingredients

4 venison steaks from the saddle, about 150g (5½oz) each

1 tbsp olive oil

50g (1¾oz) salted butter

2 tbsp port

1 tbsp balsamic vinegar

75ml (2½fl oz) chicken or game stock

mixed salad leaves, to serve

For the butternut squash mash

1 small butternut squash, peeled and cut into 5cm (2in) cubes

salt and freshly ground black pepper

2 tbsp olive oil

25g (scant 1oz) butter

Method →

Method

1 Preheat the oven to 200°C (400°F/Gas 6). Place the butternut squash into a roasting tin, season with salt and pepper, and coat with the olive oil. Roast in the oven for about 30 minutes, until crisp and tender. Then mash with the butter and keep warm.

2 To cook the venison, heat the olive oil and half of the butter in a frying pan. Sear the venison on each side and cook to taste as you would a fillet steak (about 3 minutes a side for medium rare). Set aside to rest.

TECHNIQUE

How to prepare and roast butternut squash

1 Hold the squash firmly on the board, then cut in half, cutting from the stalk end directly through the core end.

2 Use a spoon or a small ice cream scoop to remove the seeds and fibres from each squash half. Discard the seeds and fibres.

3 Add the port, balsamic vinegar, and stock to the same frying pan, and reduce until the liquid is bubbling away and about half the volume. Take off the heat and stir in the remaining butter.

4 Put the venison steaks on serving plates and add a quenelle of roasted butternut squash mash and some mixed salad leaves. Drizzle the balsamic reduction around the edge.

3 Cut the squash into sections. If you are removing the skin before cooking, peel the sections using a vegetable peeler or knife.

4 Preheat oven to 200°C (400°F, gas 6). Cut squash into small cubes. Put into a roasting tin, season, and drizzle over melted butter or oil. Roast until crisp and tender – about 30 minutes.

Carpaccio of venison with watercress salad and a raspberry vinaigrette

Angela Kenny @ semi-finalist

Preparation time 35 minutes   **Cooking time** 2 minutes   **Serves 4**

Ingredients

1 tbsp dried thyme

salt and freshly ground
black pepper

200g (7oz) loin of
venison

1 tbsp olive oil

85g (3oz) watercress

For the vinaigrette

30g (1oz) raspberries

4 tbsp balsamic vinegar

90ml (3fl oz) olive oil

Method →

Method

1 Preheat a frying pan until hot. Season the thyme with salt and pepper and spread on a plate. Rub the venison with some of the olive oil and roll it in the herb mixture.

2 Place the venison in the hot frying pan and sear all the edges. Remove from the pan and leave to rest for around 30 minutes.

3 Meanwhile, make the vinaigrette by puréeing the raspberries with a hand blender and pass through a sieve to remove any pips. Mix the raspberry purée with the balsamic vinegar and olive oil, and add salt and pepper to taste.

4 Thinly slice the venison, arrange on a serving plate and sprinkle with salt and pepper. Arrange the watercress in the centre and drizzle the dressing over the top.

How to prepare carpaccio

Preheat a frying pan until hot. Mix about 1 tbsp dried thyme with some salt and pepper and spread on a plate. Rub oil over a piece of beef fillet or venison loin, then roll it in the herb mixture. Place in the hot frying pan and sear all over. Remove from pan and leave to rest for 30 minutes. Slice meat thinly, arrange on a serving plate, and season with salt and pepper.

Pan-fried lamb's liver with pancetta and horseradish mash

Chris Gates @ finalist

Preparation time 15minutes   **Cooking time** 25 minutes   **Serves 4**

Ingredients

2 tbsp olive oil

5 pancetta slices

small bunch of sage, leaves removed

1 onion, thinly sliced

300g (10oz) lamb's liver, trimmed and sliced

plain flour, to dust

knob of salted butter

2 tbsp red wine vinegar

For the horseradish mash

3 large potatoes, peeled and chopped

salt and freshly ground black pepper

20g (¾oz) salted butter

about 2 tbsp creamed horseradish

about 100ml (3½fl oz) double cream, warmed

Method

1 For the mash, bring a large pan of salted water to the boil. Add the potatoes and simmer for about 20 minutes until soft.

2 Meanwhile, in a large frying pan heat half the oil and fry the pancetta for 4–5 minutes or until crisp. Remove from the pan and put to one side. Then fry the sage leaves until crisp and also put to one side. Finally, fry the onion for 12–15 minutes over medium-low heat until caramelized. Set aside.

3 Dust the sliced liver with a little flour. In a large frying pan, heat the remaining olive oil and fry the liver over a high heat for 1–2 minutes on each side until sealed. Return the pancetta, sage leaves, and onion to the pan. Add the knob of butter and the vinegar and heat through.

4 Drain and mash the potatoes and season with salt and pepper. Add the butter, creamed horseradish and double cream to taste.

5 Serve the horseradish mash in large bowls with the liver on top.

Pan-fried duck with salsa verde

Chris Gates @ finalist

Preparation time 15 minutes   **Cooking time** 17 minutes   **Serves 4**

Ingredients

4 duck breasts

salt and freshly ground black pepper

For the salsa verde

2 tbsp chopped capers

2 tbsp chopped gerkins

3 anchovy fillets, chopped

1 tsp Dijon mustard

1 tsp red wine vinegar

1 small bunch of basil, chopped

1 small bunch of flat-leaf parsley, chopped

1 small bunch of mint, chopped

about 90ml (3fl oz) olive oil to taste

Method

1 To cook the duck breasts, score the skin and season with salt and pepper. Place the duck skin-side down in a cold pan and cook over medium to hot heat for 10 minutes to allow the fat to render out. Turn the duck over and continue cooking for a further 6–8 minutes.

2 Mix all of the salsa verde ingredients together, loosen with the olive oil, and season to taste.

3 Serve the duck with seasonal vegetables, such as steamed green beans and carrots, tossed in the salsa verde.

Rhubarb tarte Tatin with mascarpone

Marianne Lumb @ Professionals finalist

Preparation time 15 minutes **Cooking time** 30 minutes **Serves 4**

Ingredients

200g (7oz) ready-made puff pastry

6 thick rhubarb sticks

150g (5½oz) unsalted butter, softened

125g (4½oz) granulated sugar

grated zest of 1 orange

2 vanilla pods, each split and cut into 4 pieces

200g (7oz) mascarpone cheese

Method →

Method

1 Preheat the oven to 190°C (375°F/Gas 5) and get out 4 heatproof blini pans. Roll out the puff pastry to about 3mm (⅛in) thick and cut into 4 discs with a diameter slightly larger than the pans. Prick each disc and leave to chill in the fridge.

2 Cut up the rhubarb sticks to fit into the 4 blini pans perfectly in 2 layers. Cover the base of each pan with some of the butter, sprinkle over some sugar, orange zest, and a piece of vanilla pod, and then add the rhubarb pieces.

3 Place pans over a very hight heat on the hob and cook the rhubarb for about 10 minutes to reach a good, bitter caramelization. Check by carefully lifting up the rhubarb with a palette knife, but do not be tempted to stir the rhubarb.

4 Cover each pan carefully with a disc of puff pastry, allowing the pastry to tuck just inside the pans. Place the pans on a baking sheet and bake in the hot oven for 20–30 minutes, or until the puff pastry is perfectly cooked and the tartes have a good caramelization. Remove from the oven and allow to rest for a few minutes.

5 Carefully invert each pan over a serving plate, letting the tarte drop gently down. Serve immediately, each tarte topped with a scoop of mascarpone cheese and a remaining piece of vanilla pod to decorate.

White chocolate, blueberry, and amaretto mascarpone cheesecake

Becky McCracken @ semi-finalist

Preparation time 30 minutes   **Serves 4**

Ingredients

100g (3½oz) amaretti biscuits, crushed

50g (1¾oz) unsalted butter, melted

150g (5½oz) white chocolate, broken into pieces

500g (1lb 2oz) mascarpone cheese

25g (scant 1oz) icing sugar

200g (7oz) blueberries

2 tbsp amaretto liqueur

Method

1 Mix the amaretti biscuits with the melted butter. Pack the biscuit mixture into the bases of four 8–10cm (3½–4in) ring moulds.

2 Melt the white chocolate in a bowl, set over a pan of gently simmering water. Tip the mascarpone into a large bowl, then beat in the melted chocolate. Taste the mixture. It should be sweet but not too cloying. If necessary, add some sieved icing sugar to taste.

3 Put cheese mixture on top of the biscuit bases and push some of the blueberries down into the mixture. Put in the fridge to chill for at least 1 hour.

4 To serve, gently heat the remaining blueberries in a pan with the amaretto liqueur until they just pop open. Remove cheesecakes from the moulds (you may need to soften with a kitchen blow torch or a warmed knife if they are really cold) and place on individual plates. Spoon over the hot blueberry sauce and serve immediately.

Black and redcurrant fool with ginger biscuits

Peter Thompson @ quarter-finalist

Preparation time 10 minutes   **Cooking time** 30 minutes   **Serves 4**

Ingredients

For the ginger biscuits

100g (3½oz) plain flour

1 tsp baking powder

pinch of salt

½ tsp ground cinnamon

2 tsp ground ginger

½ tsp freshly grated nutmeg

50g (1¾oz) light soft brown sugar

50g (1¾oz) crystallized ginger, finely chopped

50g (1¾oz) unsalted butter, softened

1 tbsp milk

For the fool

300g (10oz) redcurrants, plus extra to decorate

300g (10oz) blackcurrants

few drops of lemon juice

2 tbsp caster sugar

400ml (14fl oz) double cream, whipped

200g (7oz) Greek-style yogurt

Method →

Method

1 Preheat the oven to 150°C (300°F/Gas 2). Grease 2 baking sheets.

2 To make the ginger biscuits, place all the ingredients except the butter and milk in a food processor and mix together. Add the butter and milk and work together to a smooth dough.

3 Roll the dough into a sausage and chill for 20 minutes before slicing into 5mm (¼in) thick biscuits (should make about 16 of them). Place on the baking sheets and bake in the oven for 20 minutes or until golden.

4 For the fool, lightly poach the fruit in separate pans with a little water and lemon juice and sugar (1 tbsp in each). Poach for 6–8 minutes. The fruit should remain recognisable and not a be mush. It should also be reasonably sharp.

5 In a bowl, fold together the whipped cream and yogurt.

6 In each of 4 glasses, layer the black and redcurrants separately, intercut by the cream so that all 3 colours are visible. Serve with the reserved redcurrants and 2 biscuits per person, which should add the necessary sweetness. Store the remaining biscuits for a few days in an airtight container.

Saucy lemon pudding with raspberries

Matt Edwards @ semi-finalist

Preparation time 5 minutes   **Cooking time** 30–35 minutes   **Serves 6**

Ingredients

25g (scant 1oz) unsalted butter

2 large eggs, separated

250ml (8fl oz) milk

250g (9oz) caster sugar

3 tbsp flour, sifted

a pinch of sea salt

grated zest and juice of 1 unwaxed lemon

100g (3½oz) raspberries

250ml (8oz) double cream

sprigs of mint, to decorate

Method

1 Preheat the oven to 200°C (400°F/Gas 6). Grease six 200ml (7fl oz) ramekins or teacups with the butter and set aside.

2 Beat the egg yolks with the milk. Combine the sugar, flour, and salt, then pour in the milk and egg mixture and fold in the lemon juice and zest.

3 With an electric beater, whisk the egg whites to stiff peaks and fold through the lemon mixture.

4 Pour into the ramekins and poke 4–5 raspberries into the batter. Place the ramekins in a roasting tin, pour enough boiling water around them to reach about 3cm (1¼in) deep and bake for 30–35 minutes until the tops are golden and set.

5 Serve with the double cream and remaining raspberries, decorated with mint.

Strawberries with sablé biscuits and orange and lemon syllabub

James Nathan @ champion

Preparation time 40 minutes   **Cooking time** 8 minutes   **Serves 4**

Ingredients

For the sablé biscuits

100g (3½oz) plain flour

75g (2½oz) unsalted butter

100g (3½oz) golden caster sugar

grated zest of 1 lemon

2 egg yolks

For the syllabub

50g (1¾oz) caster sugar

grated zest and juice of 1 orange

grated zest and juice of 1 lemon

300ml (10fl oz) double cream

For the strawberry coulis

350g (12oz) strawberries (English if possible)

50g (1¾oz) icing sugar

3 tbsp Grand Marnier

icing sugar, for sprinkling

mint leaves

Method →

Method

1 Preheat the oven to 200°C (400°F/Gas 6). To make the biscuits, mix the flour, butter, sugar, lemon zest, and egg yolks together in a food processor until a soft ball of dough is formed. Rest in the refrigerator for about 30 minutes. Roll out thinly. Cut out 8 biscuits with a 7–8cm (2¾–3½in) pastry cutter and bake in the oven on a greased baking tray until golden, for about 6–8 minutes.

2 To make the coulis, hull 200g (7oz) of the strawberries. Purée with the icing sugar and Grand Marnier in a food processor. Check for sweetness and adjust if necessary. Pass through a fine sieve and chill the mixture until required.

TECHNIQUE

How to make sablé biscuits

1 Preheat the oven to 180°C (350°F/Gas 4) Mix 200g (7oz) each of castor sugar and sifted flour in a bowl. Rub in 150g (5½oz) butter until mixture resembles crumbs. Mix in 4 egg yolks to form a soft dough.

2 On a lightly floured surface, briefly knead the dough until smooth. Roll out to a thickness of 5mm (¼in). If needed, use a palette knife to move the sheet of dough around to prevent it sticking.

3 For the syllabub, combine the sugar and zest and juice from the orange and lemon. Whisk the cream until it forms soft peaks. Add the citrus mixture and whisk to firm peaks. Chill until required.

4 To serve, put a swirl of the coulis on each plate. Set a biscuit alongside it. Put a few spoonfuls of syllabub in the centre of the biscuit and surround with the remaining strawberries, halved lengthways to make pillars. Top with another biscuit. Sprinkle with icing sugar and add some mint leaves to finish.

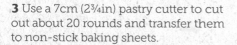

3 Use a 7cm (2¾in) pastry cutter to cut out about 20 rounds and transfer them to non-stick baking sheets.

4 Bake in batches for 10–15 minutes, until the biscuits are golden brown at the edges. Cool them on the baking sheets until firm enough to handle, then transfer to a wire rack to cool completely.

Pineapple and macadamia nut poké with rum sauce and coconut rice pudding

Tim Anderson @ champion

Preparation time 15 minutes   **Cooking time** 35 minutes   **Serves 4**

Ingredients

For the rice pudding

50g (1¾oz) Japanese short-grain rice or Arborio rice

40g (1¼oz) caster sugar

½ tsp ground cinnamon

½ tsp freshly grated nutmeg

finely grated zest of ½ orange

finely grated zest of ½ lime

300ml (10fl oz) coconut milk

300ml (10fl oz) whole milk

For the poké

50g (1¾oz) macadamia nuts, roughly chopped

1 small supersweet pineapple, peeled, cored, and diced

3 tbsp desiccated coconut

shredded zest of ½ lime

shredded zest of ½ orange

For the sauce

50g (1¾oz) butter

75g (2½oz) light soft brown sugar

1 vanilla pod, split and seeds scraped out

1 tbsp dark rum

Method

Method

1 First cook the coconut rice pudding. Combine the rice, sugar, cinnamon, nutmeg, orange and lime zests, coconut milk, and whole milk in a saucepan and bring to the boil. Reduce the heat and simmer gently, uncovered, for 25 minutes, stirring continuously until the rice is soft and creamy. Add a little extra milk if the pudding begins to dry out. Cover with a circle of wet greaseproof paper to prevent a skin forming. Set aside.

2 Make the poké. Toast the macadamia nuts in a dry frying pan for a few minutes, shaking the pan all the time until lightly golden. Remove from the heat immediately to prevent them burning and transfer them to a bowl. Add the diced pineapple. Toss together to mix well.

TECHNIQUE

How to cut a pineapple

1 With a sharp knife, cut the top and the base from the pineapple. Stand the pineapple upright and cut along the contour of the flesh, removing the skin in long strips from top to bottom.

2 To make rings, turn the pineapple sideways and cut it into slices of an even thickness. Then use a round metal cutter to remove the hard, fibrous centre of each ring.

3 In the same dry frying pan, toast the desiccated coconut until golden brown, stirring all the time, being careful not to let it burn. Transfer immediately to a plate and set aside.

4 To make the rum sauce, melt the butter over medium heat, then stir in the brown sugar and cook until the sugar has melted completely. Stir in the seeds from the vanilla pod, then remove from the heat. Add the rum and ignite. Gently swirl the pan until the flames subside.

5 Remove the paper from the rice pudding and transfer it into a glass bowl, then pour on the vanilla rum sauce. Top with the poké of nuts and pineapple, then the toasted coconut. Sprinkle the shredded lime and orange zests over the top.

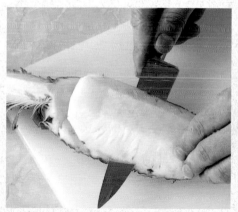 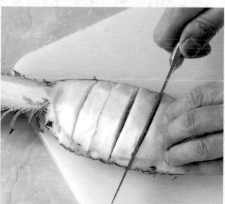

3 To slice, first quarter the fruit by cutting from plume end to base, then cut out and remove the core at the centre of each piece. Beginning at the plume end, cut along between the flesh and the skin.

4 Hold the pineapple steady and cut the flesh crossways against the skin, making slices of an even width. Repeat with the other quarters. To make dice or cubes, cut lengthways down each row of slices.

Index

Acknowledgments

Shine TV and Endemol Shine Group would like to thank:
Frances Adams, David Ambler, Alice Bernardi, Martin Buckett, Claire Burton, Bev Comboy, Kerisa Edwards, Jessica Hannan, Ozen Kazim, Angela Loftus, Lou Plank, Lyndsey Posner, Franc Roddam, John Torode, and Gregg Wallace.

MasterChef alumni whose recipes and quotes are reproduced in this book:
Tim Anderson, Annie Assheton, Dhruv Baker, Natalie Brenner, Susie Carter, Alice Churchill, David Coulson, Helen Cristofoli, Lisa Faulkner, Andrew Fletcher, Chris Gates, Ruth Goodman, Steve Groves, Christine Hamiliton, Gary Heath, Jackie Kearney, Tim Kinnaird, Hannah Miles, Daksha Mistry, Perveen Nekoo, Wendi Peters, Nick PIckard, Alex Rushmer, Dennice Russell, Nadia Sawalha, Jenny Shanks, Stacie Stewart, Dick Strawbridge, Alice Taylor, Rachel Thompson, Midge Ure, Kirsty Wark, Gillian Wylie, and Adam Young.

Dorling Kindersley would like to thank:
Libby Brown and Amy Slack for editorial assistance, Philippa Nash for design assistance, and Vanessa Bird for indexing.

Senior Editor Cécile Landau
Senior Art Editor Alison Shackleton
Managing Editor Stephanie Farrow
Managing Art Editor Christine Keilty
Jacket Designer Steven Marsden
Producer, Pre-Production Robert Dunn
Producer Stephanie McConnell
Special Sales Creative Project Manager
Alison Donovan
Art Director Maxine Pedliham
Publisher Mary-Clare Jerram

First published in Great Britain in 2018 by
Dorling Kindersley Limited, 80 Strand, London, WC2R 0RL
A Penguin Random House Company

Material previous published in:
The MasterChef Cookbook (2010), MasterChef At Home (2011),
MasterChef Kitchen Bible (2011),
and MasterChef Everyday (2012)

10 9 8 7 6 5 4 3 2 1
001—309618—Feb/2018

A CIP catalogue record for this book is available
from the British Library.
ISBN 978-0-2413-3335-8